HOUGHTON MIFFLIN

Reading

A Legacy of Literacy

Journeys

 HOUGHTON MIFFLIN   BOSTON · MORRIS PLAINS, NJ

California · Colorado · Georgia · Illinois · New Jersey · Texas

Design, Art Management and Page Production: Kirchoff/Wohlberg, Inc.

ILLUSTRATION CREDITS
4-21 Phil Boatwright. **22-39** Sandra Speidel. **40-45, 47-48, 50, 52, 57** Paul Lee. **58-75** Winson Trang.

PHOTOGRAPHY CREDITS
40 The Mariner's Museum, Newport News VA. **46** Peabody Essex Museum, Salem MA. Photo By Mark Sexton. **49, 51, 53, 54, 55, 56, 57** Milt Butterworth.

Printed in U.S.A.

ISBN: 0-618-04398-5

11 12 13 14 - VH - 06 05 04 03

Journeys

Contents

Sky **4**
by Julia Hanna
illustrated by Phil Boatwright

Elena in America **22**
by Robin Bloksberg
illustrated by Sandra Speidel

**Tommy Thompson's Ship
of Gold** **40**
by Anne Sibley O'Brien
illustrated by Paul Lee

Race of the *River Runner* **58**
by Geoff Smith
illustrated by Winson Trang

Sky

by Julia Hanna
illustrated by Phil Boatwright

Strategy Focus

It's roundup time. What dangers lay ahead for Sky and his partner, Rick? As you read, stop to **summarize** parts of the story.

Sky pulled hard against the reins in his
partner's hands. "Easy, boy," said Rick. The
spring Wyoming air filled Sky's nose. The
roundup was just starting. For the first time,
Sky would help.

The roundup took place each year. Cowboys led wild horses back to the ranch. From there the horses would be sent to new homes. That was how Rick had found Sky.

The roundup wasn't like the work Sky had done on the ranch. Things happened faster than a jack rabbit on fire. Sky knew herding wild horses could be dangerous.

Chop-chop-whirrr! The helicopter zoomed too low. A mare and her foal jumped from the herd. Sky felt Rick jerk the reins. In a flash they were after the mare.

The mare and her foal were faster than any ornery cow in the barnyard. The ground was rough here too. Sky tried to keep up, but a hole changed his plans.

Sky jumped up, a little stiff but not lame. The mare and her foal were getting away! Sky watched Rick limp slowly to him. With a quick tug on the reins they were off again.

Sky wanted to gallop like greased lightning. But they were heading down into a canyon. Sky's hooves slid on the steep path. "Easy, boy!" Sky heard Rick say. "We'll find her soon enough."

At last Sky spotted the mare and the foal. They were stopped at the canyon bottom. Sky slowed to a trot. He knew not to spook the mare. But what had made her stop?

As Sky inched closer, thunder rumbled in the distance. "Move it, boy," he heard Rick say. "Storm's coming." But Sky jerked still. He started backing up.

"Knock it off," Rick said. "This isn't the rodeo."

Sky started walking in a circle. Something on the ground was rattling! Suddenly a rattlesnake slid under Sky's legs and out of sight.

"Sorry, partner," Rick said. "Guess you know what you're doing better than I do."

Sky crept to the mare. Sky was keeping her calm. After Rick caught her with his rope, Sky turned and headed up the steep canyon path.

As they climbed the canyon wall, thunder boomed closer and closer. Lightning hit all around. A tree burst into flames. The mare turned to run. But the path was too narrow.

Sky dug his hooves into the path. The mare was going to pull them over the side! The mare snorted in the air. Sky snorted back. With all his strength, he pulled against the rope.

The tree blazed hotter than a blacksmith's forge. The mare wouldn't turn. Sky could feel Rick pulling, too. The moment seemed to last forever. Finally they yanked her around and rode on.

Sky led the horses around one bend after another. With one final lunge, they popped up onto the mesa. The herd rumbled in the distance, just a few miles from the ranch.

"Well done, partner," Sky heard Rick say.

The rain began to pour. The big, cool drops felt good against Sky's dusty, hot coat. All was well now. Soon they'd be home.

Responding

Think About the Selection

1. What does Sky do for the first time?

2. Why do you think a roundup of wild horses could be dangerous?

3. Write three things Sky does after the mare and her foal run off. Write them in the correct order.

Story Structure

Complete this story map on a piece of paper by writing in the Problem, Major Events, and Outcome.

Title	*Sky*			
Setting	*out West*			
Characters	*Sky and Rick*			
Problem	?			
Major Events	?	?	?	?
Outcome	?			

Elena in America

by Robin Bloksberg

illustrated by Sandra Speidel

Will Elena be happy when she goes to America? As you read, try to **predict** how Elena will feel about her new home.

When Elena was little, she lived in Russia. Russia is a very big country. Even so, Elena's own world was small. All she knew was the little village where she and her family lived.

Then, when Elena was nine, her father told her, "Elena, we're moving to America."

When Elena's family first arrived in America, they stayed with her uncle in Evanston, Illinois.

Evanston looked nothing like Russia!

Elena felt very shy when she went into town.
The people looked different from the people she knew
in Russia. Everything seemed strange. Elena felt like
a stranger. Being a stranger was no fun.

Then, one day, Elena's father went to a nearby city. When he came back, he had a new job. "We're moving," he told the family — in Russian, of course.

So Elena's family packed their things, again, and moved to Chicago.

Elena's father started his new job. Elena spent the rest of the summer exploring the city with her mother and sister. When they spoke Russian to each other, people would sometimes stare.

It was not easy getting used to her new home.

In Russia, Elena had lived in a little town. There were few people. She knew everyone. In Chicago, there were so many people! Elena and her family didn't know anyone.

Elena wasn't sure she would be happy in America.

In September, Elena started school. She was very nervous. There were other children at school from different countries. A boy named Ivan was also from Russia! It felt wonderful for Elena to talk with him in Russian.

At Elena's school in Russia, she had had lots of friends. At her new school, Elena only knew Ivan at first. They did many things together. When Ivan was not around, Elena felt lonely.

Sometimes Elena went walking with her mother and sister. One day, they found a Russian grocery store! They bought some dark bread and delicious sausage, just like they used to eat in Russia.

Another day, Elena's mother took her to eat hamburgers. They also had milk shakes and french fries. Elena loved the food! They didn't have places like this in her little village in Russia.

Ivan was a good friend, but sometimes Elena missed having girlfriends. Then she tried out for the basketball team.

She was very proud when she made the team!

She was even happier when the team members hugged her.

Some of the girls on the basketball team became good friends to Elena. When she made mistakes in English, they helped her learn to say things the right way.

As Elena's English got better, it was easier to make new friends. Some of the girls invited her to see a movie. Elena had not laughed so much since she had left Russia. She even understood most of it!

One night, Elena invited her new friends to sleep over at her house. As a treat, her mother made them dumplings filled with meat. The girls liked them. Elena told them they were called *piroshki*.

Sometimes Elena dreams about Russia, her beautiful country. She can still picture the river that ran through the town where she lived. She can remember the taste of the salted fish she loved so well.

Elena will always be a Russian girl. But she is also starting to feel like an American girl. Elena feels as if she has two homes — the one she left behind, and the beautiful one that she now loves.

Responding

Think About the Selection

1. Where does Elena come from?

2. Why does Elena think about her village in Russia?

3. Does the author feel it is easy or hard to move to a new country? How can you tell?

What Does the Author Feel?

Copy the chart on a piece of paper. Then fill in details from the story that support what the author feels.

The Author Feels	I Know This from These Details in the Story
It feels bad to be a stranger.	The author says that being a stranger was no fun.
Having friends can make you feel good.	?
Having two countries can be nice.	?

TOMMY THOMPSON'S SHIP OF GOLD

by Anne Sibley O'Brien
illustrated by Paul Lee

Strategy Focus

A ship full of gold lies deep at the bottom of the sea. Can Tommy Thompson find the treasure? As you read, **monitor** how well you understand each part of the story.

THE SHIP SAILS, 1857

On a sunny September day in 1857, the sidewheel steamer *Central America* set sail. She was heading from Cuba to New York City. She carried over 500 people. The *Central America* also carried gold—over one-and-a-half million dollars' worth!

Two nine-year-old girls traveled on the *Central America*. Their names were Harriet Lockwood and Augustine Pahud. On this bright day, the girls laughed and played on the deck in the sun.

The Storm

Soon the skies turned dark. Wild winds started to blow. Powerful waves tossed the *Central America* like a cork. Harriet and Augustine ran inside to ride out the storm.

Before long, the crew was spreading the bad news. The *Central America* was leaking! People bailed water, trying to keep the ship from sinking.

Another ship, the *Marine*, had been spotted nearby. It was now on its way. But would it reach the *Central America* in time?

The Rescue

The *Marine* finally arrived. The *Central America* lowered her lifeboats onto the water. Harriet and Augustine went with the other children and women. The lifeboats set off through the waves for the waiting *Marine*.

This painting shows how an artist in 1857 imagined the sinking of the *Central America*.

The Ship Sinks

When the girls arrived safely on the deck of the *Marine,* they looked back at the *Central America.* Several hundred men were still on board. Many were rich miners returning from the California Gold Rush country. The girls thought how luck was about to run out for these men.

After two days, the *Central America* went down. Over 400 people, mostly men, went with her. The *Central America* also took 42,000 pounds of gold to the ocean floor. It would be over 100 years before another person saw this treasure fit for a king.

The Explorer, 1986

In 1986, Tommy Thompson was a smart young inventor who loved exploring the ocean. He dreamed of uncovering the secrets of the deep. Of all the ocean's secrets, shipwrecks interested Tommy most of all.

Tommy had heard about the *Central America*. He knew the ship had gone down with millions, maybe billions, of dollars' worth of gold. The gold would be much more valuable today than it had been in 1857. No one had ever found an underwater treasure that big.

Tommy Thompson stands on the *Arctic Discoverer*.

THE PROBLEM

Tommy also knew the *Central America* lay over one mile below the sea. Even if he could find the treasure, Tommy could never bring it up from that far down. But Tommy had a plan.

one mile

THE SOLUTION

By 1988, Tommy had made a new robot for exploring deep under the ocean. It was called a remote-operated vehicle, or ROV. Tommy could send it thousands of feet underwater to find the *Central America.*

The ROV that Tommy and his team invented, called *Nemo*.

Tommy could run the ROV from a ship called the *Arctic Discoverer.* The ROV would send pictures from the ocean floor to the ship. It could also pick up things on the ocean floor — things like gold coins.

Looking for the Central America

In the fall of 1988, Tommy and the *Arctic Discoverer* set sail to find the *Central America*. It would be the first time he used the new ROV. It had taken years of hard work and planning to get ready for this trip.

A photograph of a bell at the *Central America* wreck site, taken by *Nemo*.

Out at sea, the ROV worked better than Tommy had dreamed. On the first dive, it found the *Central America*! There were cups and plates and trunks of clothes. There were even books that could still be read.

TREASURE!

But most amazing of all, there was gold—thousands of gold coins and gold bars! Everywhere the ROV looked, there was gold. That first trip, the ROV pulled up just 40 coins. But Tommy would make more trips. Over time, he would pull up millions of dollars' worth of gold.

Everywhere they looked, Tommy's team saw gold.

Tommy used a number of inventions to pull up all the gold and other things from the *Central America*. But for Tommy, the bigger treasure was how he had solved his problem. He had found a new way to uncover the secrets hidden deep at the bottom of the sea.

Responding

1. What was the *Central America* carrying?

2. Why did the girls think the miners from California had run out of luck?

3. How do the headings help you understand what you are reading?

TEXT ORGANIZERS

Copy the chart on a piece of paper. Then for each heading in the story, tell what happened in that part of the story.

Heading	What this part of the story is about
The Ship Sails, 1857	In 1857, the *Central America* sets sail.
The Storm	A big storm hits the *Central America.*
The Rescue	?

Race of the RIVER RUNNER

by Geoff Smith
illustrated by Winson Trang

Strategy Focus

The captain of the *River Runner* takes Sun on an amazing journey. As you read, think of **questions** about the story that you might ask a friend.

SUN LIU followed his father across the busy
New York City docks. Horses pulled carts.
Workmen carried heavy sacks.

The great steamboat *River Runner* was about
to sail up the Hudson River.

Sun's father was heading to Albany on business. At the last minute, he had asked Sun to come along. On board the ship, Sun's father went right to his room to work. But Sun set off to explore.

Sun zipped up the stairs to the very top deck. It was like standing on a mountain. The blue water sparkled in the morning light. Sun wished his father could see how beautiful it was.

"What's your name, sailor?" a voice boomed.

Sun turned to see a giant man smiling right at him.

"I'm Francis Skiddy," said the man, "the pilot of this fine ship. Come on into my house."

"The best thing about life on a steamboat is that everyone is coming from or going to somewhere else," said Captain Skiddy. "What's your story?" His smile glowed like the buttons on his jacket.

Sun explained that he had been born in China. But because of his father's work, his family had moved to London, then Boston, and now New York. "I don't know where to call home," said Sun.

"I've lived on boats all my life. I'll tell you one thing I've learned," Captain Skiddy said. "Keep your eyes open and remember what you see, and you'll always carry your home with you."

Sun sat on an old, empty apple crate. The big man turned the boat's huge wooden wheel. His hands were as hard and red as two big bricks. As he steered, the captain told about life on the river.

Just before lunch another steamboat pulled up next to them.

"It's the *Hudson Queen*!" said Captain Skiddy. "She's as close to us as peel on an apple. Looks like she wants a race. What do you think, Sun?"

"Yes!" cried Sun.

Captain Skiddy sounded the whistle.

"Yell into that pipe," shouted the captain. "Tell the engine room Full Steam Ahead!"

Sun stood on his toes and yelled. The engine began to chug.

Black smoke poured from the stacks of both boats. Orange sparks flew into the air. Huge wakes of water splashed along the shore. People on both boats cheered. The race was on!

As the *River Runner* pulled ahead, people on land stopped to watch. The sight of the two steaming giants fighting it out was too good to miss. A man rode his bicycle along the shore trying to keep up.

The *River Runner's* side wheel chopped the water. But the *Hudson Queen* chugged by her side.

"Rocks ahead!" Captain Skiddy suddenly yelled. "They're trying to get us to stop short! What do you say we do, Sun?"

"More steam!" Sun yelled. Something about Captain Skiddy made him feel brave.

The *River Runner's* engine roared. The rocks lay straight ahead!

At the last moment, the captain spun the wheel. The *River Runner* shot in front of the *Hudson Queen*. The other boat turned into calm waters and slowed.

"I'd say we got her good," Skiddy laughed.

"I'd say so!" Sun cheered.

The *River Runner* pulled up to Albany later that night. The moon sat fat and bright in the black sky. As he left the boat, Sun thanked the Captain for a story that he would always carry with him.

Responding

THINK ABOUT THE SELECTION

1. What kind of boat was the *River Runner*?

2. How do you think Sun feels about Captain Skiddy at the end of the story? Why?

3. What details in the story make the steamboat race exciting?

NOTING DETAILS

Copy this web on a piece of paper. Then add two more details that describe Captain Skiddy.

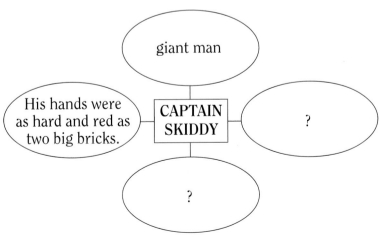

giant man

His hands were as hard and red as two big bricks.

CAPTAIN SKIDDY

?

?